MISSIONARY IDEALS

STUDIES IN THE
ACTS OF THE APOSTLES

By the Rev. T. WALKER of Tinnevelly
Edited by David C. C. Watson

INTER-VARSITY PRESS
39 Bedford Square, London WC1

First IVF edition 1938
Reprinted 1941, 1950, 1953, 1955, 1959
Second edition 1969

STANDARD BOOK NUMBER 85110 530 0

Made and printed in England by Green & Co.
(Lowestoft) Ltd., Crown Street, Lowestoft

CONTENTS

INTRODUCTION

' How much are you asking for that?' I enquired recently in a South Indian antique shop. ' Oh, I'm sorry, but that's not for sale. I wouldn't part with **him** for money !' 'That' was a portrait of the author of this book, and the dealer's reply a sample of the esteem and affection in which Walker 'Iyer' was still held, fifty-four years after his death, in the land for which he laboured. Most of his literary work was done in Tamil, of which he had acquired a rare mastery, but 'Missionary Ideals ' was written for the Church Missionary Society in Britain. Its usefulness has been proved over half a century and far beyond the bounds of one denomination, because Walker combined true scholarship with first-hand practical experience of the mission field. He himself regarded this book as ' bread and milk ' for babes, but most readers will find that it calls for hard work and hard thinking.

Walker shunned publicity almost as much as the author of Acts. He did not found a Mission or start a Movement. He was never mauled by a lion or clubbed by cannibals or pursued by Simbas. But for run-of-the-mill Christians who keep the ' noiseless tenor of their way ' along unromantic paths his life-story is a challenge and inspiration. A few examples, culled from his biography by Amy Carmichael, must suffice.

Like Henry Martyn, Walker went up to

St. John's College, Cambridge, and took the Mathematical Tripos; but, unlike him, he just failed to secure a place as a Wrangler (1882). The disappointment was turned to good account in later years, enabling him to sympathize with missionaries who failed their Tamil exams! But there was success of another kind: 'While at Cambridge Walker well and truly laid the foundations on which his future life and work were to be built. There, plain to us all, was the stern denial of self and the absolute severance from worldly amusements. He was forming the habits of devotion, prayer, and systematic Bible study, which have borne fruit in his valued Bible readings. There was the mental training, and the storing of the memory with all that would render the man of God thoroughly furnished unto every good work.' 'I was saved from theology' was a favourite quip of his when training Indian ordinands; but that did not prevent him heading the list in both Ordination Examinations.

The following quotations from his own letters, and from the testimony of friends, show how Walker as a missionary exemplified many of the ideals here set forth:

Earnestness. 'They were wondering at the intense earnestness of the speaker. That, rather than what he said, had struck and impressed them.'

Catholicity. 'I would never ask any converted man to join my church. Christ sent me to catch fish, not to steal sheep.'

Loyalty. 'In God's work it oftens happens that you have to choose between loyalty to His cause and popularity among fellow-workers.'

Disinterestedness. 'We do not wish to allow money matters to interfere with our work for God. . . . I am not going to let money considerations influence my mind in any way.'

Preaching. 'The combined scholarship, clearness of exposition, and deep spiritual power, made a great impression on me; and few men have helped me as much as he.'

Humility. 'His self-effacement was very marked. . . . I always found him scrupulously careful to conform to the rules of comity and church order in all his work.'

Separation. 'I dare not appear before God with the responsibility incurred by frittering away my days in such puerilities.'

Conservatism. 'We greatly need men of his type who are firmly fixed on the Rock of the Supreme Authority of the Bible.'

Evangelism. 'I feel more and more strongly that it is not enough just to move around preaching. We need to get hold of individual souls, and to that end we need the divine power of the Holy Ghost.'

Prayer. 'Better, far better, do less work, if need be, that we may pray more; because work done by the rushing torrent of human energy will not save a single soul : whereas work done in vital and unbroken contact with the living God will tell for all eternity.'

But the strongest impression left upon the reader is of Walker's intense dissatisfaction with himself and the work already accomplished, his ardent reaching out to the things which are before. Truly of him might the epitaph have been written, **Nil actum credens dum quid superesset agendum** (' reckoning that nothing had been done, so long as there remained anything to be done ').

Today the unfinished task of evangelizing the world is even more stupendous than in Walker's time. Millions more bow down to wood and stone, and Victorian prophecies of the speedy evangelization of India have been decently interred and forgotten. Some doors have closed to the gospel, but many others stand open still. And is not the grand message of Acts just this : that those who are willing to toil and suffer as the apostles toiled and suffered shall surely reap as great a spiritual harvest as they? For ' God has given the Holy Spirit to those who **obey** him.'

We conclude with some lines which deeply influenced Walker in his early years :

The voice of my departed Lord, ' Go! teach all nations !'
Comes on the night air and awakes mine ear.
Why stay here ? the vows of God are on me, and I may
*   no longer stop*
To play with shadows or pluck earthly flowers,
Till I my work have done and rendered up account.
And I will go; I may no longer doubt to give up friends
And idle hopes, and every tie that binds my heart to thee
*   my country.*

HOW TO USE THIS BOOK The passages listed at the head of each chapter should be read through first, followed by a quick reading of the chapter itself. Then carefully compare the text of Scripture with the comments made, and answer the questions placed alongside the text. A large-scale map of Paul's journeys is essential. If all members of the group do not have

time for all the ' Questions for further study ',
it is suggested that these be divided among
them, and each member lead a discussion
on one question.

David C. C. Watson
Coonoor, South India

OUTLINE OF THE BOOK OF THE ACTS

1-7 Witnesses in Jerusalem

1 First preparations : witnesses prepared
2 First ingathering : witnesses anointed
3 First miracle : witnesses accredited
4 First conflict : witnesses imprisoned
5 First stripes : witnesses beaten
6 First deacons : witnesses multiplied
7 First martyr : witnesses persecuted

8-12 Witnesses in all Judaea and Samaria

8 A new advance : Samaria
9 A new apostle : Paul
10 A new departure : Cornelius
11 A new centre : Antioch
12 A new struggle : Herod

**13-28 Witnesses unto the uttermost part
of the earth**

Paul's first missionary journey (SE Asia Minor)

13 A missionary call
14 A missionary circuit
15 A missionary conference

Paul's second missionary journey (Eastern Europe)

16 Three typical converts
17 Three typical cities
18 Three typical experiences

Paul's third missionary journey (Roman Asia)

19 A missionary centre
20 A missionary charge
21 A missionary crisis

Paul's fourth missionary journey (Caesarea to Rome)

22 Witnessing to the people
23 Witnessing before the council
24
25 } Witnessing before the governors
26 Witnessing before kings
27 Witnessing on board ship
28 Witnessing in a city

1 GOD'S MISSIONARY PLAN

There is nothing in the world worth living for but doing good and finishing God's work — doing the work that Christ did.

David Brainerd

Passages for study

Acts 1 : 1-14; 8; 10;
11 : 19-26; 13 : 1-4;
16 : 6-10; 23 : 11;
28 : 16-31.

The history of the Acts of the Apostles is the record of the elucidation of one supreme purpose, the evangelization of the world. The more closely we study it in detail, the more clearly it is seen to dominate every feature of the history. Everything in the book is subordinated to it, and made to subserve it in the most distinct manner possible. If once we grasp the fact that this missionary purpose is the very soul of the narrative, determining for Luke the choice of his material, suggesting the plan of his arrangement and shaping throughout the structure of his narrative, we shall see that the Acts of the Apostles is one of the most beautifully harmonious and consistent books in all the world. In our next chapter we shall see how fully the great adversary, Satan, realized this dominating purpose, and set himself to try and thwart it with all his might and main.

1 THE PLAN OF THE BOOK

It is usual to divide the book into three parts, following the lines laid down by our Lord Himself in 1 : 8. Thus we have (1) **Acts in Jerusalem**, 1-7; (2) **Acts in all Judaea and Samaria**, 8-12; and (3) **Acts in other lands**, ' unto the uttermost parts of the earth ',

13-28. This, undoubtedly, is the main plan of the book, and shows us the gospel spreading further and further, like circular waves propagated from a centre and growing larger and larger till they reach the distant shore. In particular, Acts describes **the first evangelization of the Roman Empire,** comprising at that period the main portion of the civilized world, as the first great instalment of that universal dissemination of the gospel which the divine purpose had in view. The Roman Empire contained numerous provinces, some of them far from the metropolis. Chapters 1-12 tell us of the evangelization of the province of Syria-Cilicia; 13-14 (First Pauline Journey) of the occupation of the provinces of Cyprus and Galatia (Pisidian Antioch, Iconium, Lystra, Derbe); 16-18 (Second Journey) of the extension of the work to the provinces of Macedonia and Achaia; and 19-20 (Third Journey) of the dissemination of the gospel in the important province of Proconsular Asia. Thus, one by one, the provinces were occupied in the name of Jesus Christ, till Italy itself was reached. Later on we shall study the remarkable experiences which befell God's missionaries as they planted His banner in one of these great Roman provinces.

But for our present study, it will make matters easier to understand if we regard Acts as describing the laying down of a missionary railway from Jerusalem, via the various provinces of the Empire, to Rome the great metropolis. The towns and cities occupied may be likened to stations on this missionary railway.

Now in making a new railroad, wise prospectors will determine its route with chief reference to the extent of population likely to be affected, and the amount of traffic likely to be realized. In the case of this missionary railway through the Roman Empire, God's wisdom is equally apparent. Apart from the all-sea route there were two main lines of business and commerce along which traffic flowed from the East to Rome. The one may be called the overland route. It led from Antioch of Syria via Tarsus through the Cilician Gates (a pass of Mt. Taurus), past Derbe, Iconium, Pisidian Antioch, Philadelphia, Sardis and Pergamum, to Troas; thence by a short sea-passage to Neapolis; and then along the Roman route called the Egnatian Way, via Philippi and Thessalonica to Dyrrachium; from this port passengers crossed by a 'sort of tumultuous ferry' to Brindisi, and then took the Appian Way to Rome. The other principal line of travel was the part-sea route. From Antioch of Syria to Pisidian Antioch it coincided with the overland route; beyond that it proceeded via Colossae and Laodicea, direct to Ephesus; thence passengers sailed to Corinth and, crossing the Isthmus, transhipped either for Brindisi and the Appian Way or for Puteoli via the Straits of Messina.

Bearing these two great routes in mind, let us now trace in the Acts the making of God's missionary railway (using, if possible, a sketch map). Starting from Jerusalem, it is carried first through Judaea and Samaria, on and on to Syrian Antioch (1-12). Proceeding from Antioch, as a new terminus, we follow it (13, 14) via Cyprus to Pisidian Antioch, Iconium, Lystra and Derbe — all of which latter towns lay on the main route of Roman travel, save one, Lystra, and that only a few miles removed. So far, God's missionary railway, apart from Cyprus, has stations, beyond Syrian Antioch, at Derbe,

What are the main stations, in order, mentioned in this first section of the line?

Lystra, Iconium and Pisidian Antioch.

As we know from events which had already occurred in the history, a station had been made at Tarsus also. So the gospel may now follow the usual pathway of business and commerce through the Cilician Gates. In chapters 15 : 40 - 17 : 10, we find the pioneer missionaries actually pursuing this road (15 : 41 - 16 : 6) as far as Pisidian Antioch, whence a new section of the line is laid (following, nearly, the overland route described above), via Troas, Neapolis, Philippi and Thessalonica. Thus our railroad runs along the Egnatian Way as far as Thessalonica at least.

Prove this, finding chapter and verse.

We notice that our railway builders now turn southward to Berea and Athens (17 : 10-34), neither of which lay on the main routes of travel spoken of above. Here, then, is a little section of the line off the principal routes. The evangelists next proceed to Corinth (18 : 1-18), which, with its eastern port of Cenchreae, was situated on the great part-sea route to Rome. It is as though a new section of the railway were laid across the Isthmus, waiting to be linked up with Pisidian Antioch, via Ephesus. This linking up follows during Paul's Third Journey (18 : 23 - 19 : 41). He had already spent a sabbath at Ephesus prospecting (18 : 19-23). Now he pursues the old route from Antioch of Syria to Pisidian Antioch, from which he lays down the new section to Ephesus, with the result, as we know from other passages of Scripture, that stations are formed not only at Ephesus itself but also at Colossae and Laodicea along the part-sea route; and at Philadelphia, Sardis and Pergamum, which lay, as we have seen, along the main overland route (thus linking up Pisidian Antioch with Troas in the usual Roman

God had, undoubtedly, special reasons for forming this side-line. What do you think they were ? Why was Athens of special importance ?

way). So God's missionary railway is laid down, very nearly, along the double route of ordinary travel from Jerusalem to Rome.

We are struck, as we study the Acts, by the fact that the undertaking of fresh sections of the line was usually preceded by the stimulus of some new spiritual awakening, or some fresh vision of God's purpose. And it is still the same. Scores of examples of the modern working of this principle might be given, but the two following from South India will suffice.

At a large Convention of Syrian Christians in Travancore some years ago, an Indian brother, acting under the influence of a fresh stimulus of grace, extemporized some verses which were sung enthusiastically again and again by the assembled thousands :

Jesus Christ still lives to conquer.
Alleluia !
Jesus Christ shall conquer India.
Alleluia !

The practical outcome of such enthusiasm, fostered since by various means, was a new section of God's railway opened in India by those same Syrian Christians in a hitherto unevangelized district of North Kanara on the west coast.

Again, an unconverted and worldly-minded Christian from Jaffna in North Ceylon was brought into personal contact with a saintly American missionary of Bombay. The result was a total transformation of life and character. With the assistance of his godly wife, he stirred up the Jaffna Christians to form a small missionary society, which took up work in a neglected part of the east coast of India. That led, in turn, to the stirring up of a well-known Tinnevelly

Christian to start the Indian Missionary Society, which is now working vigorously and with good success in many places. Who can tell where a fresh spiritual impetus will end ?

It is interesting to observe that Luke mentions by name those, and only those, whose actions directly affect this missionary plan and purpose. In particular, he considers Christian workers of importance only in so far as they have to do with the supreme purpose of the evangelization of the world. Individual missionaries and evangelists are visible to view only so long as they are busy in the forward movement. Many of them doubtless did good work as ' apostles of the circumcision ' or as pastors of churches; but Luke has no further place for them in his narrative when they cease to construct fresh sections of the missionary railway.

During the initial stage of railway construction in Jerusalem and the vicinity (chapters 1-5), Peter and John, as the chief pioneer workers, occupy the foreground of the picture. Then Stephen becomes the central figure (chapters 6-7), because of his missionary outlook and catholic sympathies, and because his martyrdom led to a wide extension of the railway. He is followed by Philip the Evangelist, for the simple reason that he carried the railway forward through Samaria and beyond (chapter 8). His figure then fades from view (save for one significant incident), to make room for Paul, the great missionary to the Gentiles, whose conversion and first labours are purposely dwelt upon (9 : 1-31). Notice, in this connection, the brief appearance of Ananias on the scene.

Peter next reappears, clearly because he

2 THE PERSONNEL OF THE BOOK

Why, as regards our missionary railway, are they mentioned again in chapter 8 ?

Show, from his work and speech, that he projected such extensions.

B

opens a new section of the railway for the Gentiles at Caesarea (9 : 32 - 11 : 18). (He is mentioned again in chapter 12 because, as in chapter 8, fresh persecution led to a fresh forward movement; see verse 24.) He makes room, in turn, for unnamed evangelists and for Barnabas (11 : 19-24), as they carry the railway to Antioch of Syria, the great foreign missions centre from that time forward. The narrative is next concerned with the apostles Paul and Barnabas (11 : 25-30; 12 : 24 - 15 : 39), as they push ahead into South Galatia. (Notice when, and for how long, John Mark is mentioned.) Henceforth Barnabas disappears from view, and the events of the Second Journey group themselves round Paul, Silas and Timothy. Apollos (18 : 24-28) is seen for a passing moment, but the rest of the narrative is concerned entirely with Paul and his companions.

Why are Peter and James referred to, from the extension point of view, in chapter 15 ?

Why ? What causes led to his being side-tracked ?

Who were these companions ? Where are they mentioned ? What part did they take in the forward movement ?

Enough has been said, surely, to prove that Luke's notices of individual workers are entirely governed by their connection with the extension of the gospel. Is God judging our lives at all in the same way? We shall reserve for another chapter our consideration of the special qualifications required in these railway pioneers. For the present, the great matter is to emphasize the paramount importance of using our best endeavours in furtherance of the gospel.

In the Tinnevelly district of South India there is a large Hindu temple situated on the sea-coast. Thousands and tens of thousands of pilgrims flock there from all parts. It is built of stone, which had to be transferred for a considerable distance over wide wastes of heavy sand. It is said that, in order to transport the material under such difficult circumstances, the Hindus of those days formed themselves into a long line, stretching for miles over the desert sands. The stones were then handed from one to the other till they passed from end to end of that human chain and were finally put in place, till the temple was finished and its ' gopura ' or tower rose conspicuous for miles around. The illustration forcibly reminds us Christians of our duty as regards the fulfilment of God's great missionary plan.

The miracles and other supernatural phenomena in the book will also be found to be regulated entirely by God's missionary purpose. All have a distinct evangelistic value. In this they contrast forcibly with such spurious phenomena as sometimes come to notice in the mission-field. To mention only one : after a time of revival in a Tinnevelly Christian congregation, some mysterious and undecipherable characters, claimed to be miraculous, appeared on the inner wall of a Christian house. They attracted great attention, and crowds of people flocked to see and wonder at them. Much curiosity was aroused, but no interest in the gospel. **They had no evangelistic value.** It needed only the lapse of time to reveal the fact that they had been inscribed on the wall by the owner of the house in a moment of frenzy and excitement when he was practically unconscious of what he did. Far otherwise is it with the real and genuine phenomena of the Acts of the Apostles which always have a direct bearing on the advance and furtherance of the gospel.

Take, for instance, **the gift of tongues,** as it is commonly called. This is not mentioned as bestowed indiscriminately, without reference to special occasions or objects. We read three times in Acts of men ' speak-

3 THE SUPERNATURAL PHENOMENA OF THE BOOK

ing with tongues ' (chapters 2; 10; 19); and on each occasion the gift was vouchsafed with a missionary object, on the threshold of a special extension of the gospel. The first occasion was that of the Pentecost of the Jews; the second that of the Pentecost of the Gentiles; and the third that of the inauguration of very special work in Proconsular Asia which led to the foundation of the seven churches of Asia with world-wide results of blessing. Thus the gift in question was, so to speak, God's special imprimatur bestowed at critical moments on new departures in missionary work.

Or think of **the visions** of the Acts. We shall not find a single one which has not a directly missionary bearing. Nine are specifically mentioned (7 : 55; 9 : 5 and parallels; 9 : 10; 10 : 3; 10 : 11; 16 : 9; 18 : 9; 22 : 17; 23 : 11), every one of them leading immediately to the wider dissemination of the gospel. The same may be said of the five **angelic interpositions** recorded in the book.

Look them out, and find their evangelistic value.

Or we may consider **the miracles** of the story, which do not occur haphazardly, but are, in every case, God's special credentials given to encourage fresh steps of missionary enterprise. We meet with them in 2 : 43; 3 : 7, 8; 5 : 1-16; 6 : 8; 8 : 6-13; 9 : 33-42; 13 : 11; 14 : 10; 16 : 18, 26; 19 : 11, 12; 20 : 9, 10; 28 : 8-10; and we may observe that they were wrought almost invariably at some critical juncture of a directly forward movement. There is only one apparent exception to this rule and even that may be shown to have an important missionary value.

Which is it ?

4 THE PARTICULAR EVENTS OF THE BOOK

Luke's choice of material was plainly regulated by the great missionary purpose of Acts. Why does he omit some things which we should have considered important? Why, again, does he dwell in detail on many things which an ordinary church historian would have omitted or very briefly noticed? Here is a fruitful field for study, but only a few illustrations can be cited, by way of suggestion.

In the matter of church organization, he mentions indeed the appointment of the seven deacons (chapter 6), but chiefly because of the work of Stephen and Philip in which it resulted and the Christian dispersion which ensued. But he introduces the order of elders or presbyters abruptly, without describing either its origin or functions (11 : 30). Why is this ? Surely because he considers evangelization of vastly greater importance than organization, urgently necessary though this may be.

Again, in narrating the history of Paul, his special friend, hero and companion, he tells us nothing of his constantly recurring malady and comparatively little of his manifold and great sufferings for the gospel's sake. We have to look elsewhere for detailed information about these. He is silent, too, about the apostle's retirement to Arabia and many other facts of his personal history mentioned in the Epistles. The reason is obvious. He is writing not the biography of a great missionary but the account of a missionary enterprise, and everything is omitted which has not a direct bearing on the object in view.

2 Cor. 1; 11, etc.

Gal. 1 : 17.

Notice, among many other things, the great length at which Stephen's speech is recorded; the fullness of the Cornelius narrative; the importance attached to Paul's address at Pisidian Antioch; the brevity of the account of the work at Derbe and Berea; the detailed history of the Ephesian episodes; the unusual diffusiveness of chapters

22-28. Our sense of proportion will be satisfied only when we weigh each particular event recorded in Luke's scales. Writing under divine inspiration he had only one object before him, the elucidation and illustration of God's grand missionary purpose.

QUESTIONS FOR FURTHER STUDY

1 Show how the following objections are completely answered by the general teaching of the Acts of the Apostles:

(a) 'It is wrong to send missionaries abroad when there are so many heathen at home.'
(b) 'We should not interfere with the pious beliefs of the followers of other religions.'
(c) 'Prayer and work are needed far more for the deepening of the spiritual life of the home church than for missionary work abroad.'

2 What is there in other books of the New Testament to show that the primary purpose of the church's existence is to evangelize the world?

3 What instances occur in Acts of Christians being scattered by persecution and so spreading the faith?

4 Is the occupation of strategic centres more important or more scriptural than the evangelization of village districts?

2 THE MISSIONARY'S ADVERSARY

The evangelisation of the heathen world . . . is a desperate struggle with the prince of darkness, and with everything his rage can stir up in the shape of obstacles, vexations, oppositions, and hatred, whether by circumstances or by the hand of man. Francois Coillard

From the very first, strenuous opposition was offered to the progress of the gospel. The ground was stoutly contested step by step. Motives of self-interest, racial pride, political prejudice and pagan zeal influenced men in their antagonism to the truth. But behind all these we recognize the great protagonist, Satan. Just as, on the one hand, we see all through the history the Holy Spirit directing, controlling and crowning with success the labours of His servants, so, on the other hand, we see the arch-enemy busily at work, trying to hinder and thwart in every way their earnest efforts. It was from long and bitter experience of Satan's malice that the apostle wrote, ' We are not ignorant of his devices.' Now, if we confine our study in this chapter to part 1 of the Acts (chapters 1-7), we shall find the enemy making use of **five special devices** in his determined efforts to frustrate God's missionary purpose. It will be further seen that there is a system and order in these devices. They were practised alternately from without and from within the church, and each one was intended to be more effectual than its predecessors. At the same time, each one was over-ruled by the

Passages for study

Acts 4; 5 : 1-16;
5 : 17-41; 6 : 1-8;
6 : 9 - 7 : 60; 2 Cor.
2 : 9-11; 11 : 1-3;
1 Thess. 2 : 14-20.

Give examples of each of these from the Acts.

power and wisdom of God's Spirit for the furtherance of the gospel; so that the adversary over-reached himself.

1 OPPOSITION
(Chapter 4)

We may always expect some special work of the Holy Spirit to be followed immediately by Satan's fierce opposition. The marvellous ingathering of the Day of Pentecost — with the daily conversions which followed and the further increase that ensued on the healing of the lame man — served as a direct challenge to the great adversary. At once his zeal and enmity were roused. Violent hands were laid on the two apostolic leaders. They were thrown into prison, examined before the Sanhedrin or Council, commanded to cease from preaching and threatened with severe penalties if they persisted. In this way, the adversary made a strenuous effort to silence the chief missionaries in Jerusalem, and so to check, at the outset, the extension of the work to the regions beyond.

History repeats itself. The planting of missions in other lands has frequently met with strong opposition on the very threshold of the work. Witness, for example, the foundation of the work in Burma, where Adoniram Judson was thrown into prison and grievously maltreated. In breaking up new ground in unevangelized towns and villages, various methods of antagonism are often encountered. Some of us have known opposing crowds shout vociferously by the half-hour the name of some favourite heathen deity, 'Gopal! Gopal! Gopal!' in order to drown the voice of the Christian preacher; or throw stones at our heads and cast dirt and dust in our faces in the hope of preventing conversions; or induce some one to burn chillies (strong red pepper) hard by, so as to choke the evangelists with fits of coughing; or command us peremptorily to leave the place under threat of pains and penalties.

Our narrative shows us, however, what to do with all such opposition. To the apostles it was a call to united prayer. Neither their faith nor their courage failed. They appealed to God to deal with the situation. They based their prayer on Holy Scripture, a good pattern for ourselves. They asked for exactly what they most needed under the circumstances, but not for permission to desist from their enterprise. And they prayed with the right motive, and left the threatenings and opposition at God's feet.

Why did they address Him, in the circumstances, as 'Master' or 'Despot' and as Creator? See RV margin.

What was (a) their need; (b) their motive; and what texts invite us to follow their example?

It is told of Ragland, a former Tinnevelly missionary of exceptional devotion and saintliness, that when he was preaching one day in a Brahmin street, the Brahmins were rude and noisy in their opposition, and forcibly expelled him from their quarters. It happened that the European magistrate of the district was camping in the neighbourhood and heard of this ill-treatment. He sent one of his 'peons' (servant-messengers) to Ragland and asked him to lodge a formal complaint, that he might punish the offenders. The messenger found Ragland on his knees. 'Tell your master,' said the man of God, 'that I have already made known my case to a higher Magistrate, the God of heaven Himself.' And the prayer was not in vain, for that very day the Brahmins came and begged his pardon, beseeching him to come back to their street and preach to them.

Mark in the Acts how **God over-ruled the opposition for good.** The gospel of salvation was clearly sounded in the Sanhedrin. Only as prisoners could humble men like Peter and John ever hope to witness there.

The opposition was followed, too, by a fresh out-pouring of the Holy Ghost, accompanied by marvellous results.

These should be classified.

2 DECEPTION (5 : 1-11)

Foiled in his first attempt to injure the cause **from without**, the adversary next assailed it **from within**. He sought to corrupt the infant church, and so impede its usefulness, by fostering insincerity among its members. For God's reality Satan always has his counterfeit and sham. He produces spurious converts, spurious doctrines, spurious miracles, spurious teachers and apostles.

Give one example of each from Acts or Epistles.

In this case he counterfeited **Christian consecration**. Over against Barnabas with his true offering stands Ananias with his make-believe. To all appearance the actions of the two men were the same. Both sold their land and laid their money at the apostles' feet. But, in reality, the difference between the two was as wide as that between light and darkness. The one was filled with the Holy Ghost; the other was filled with Satan. The one was a saint; the other was a hypocrite. Moreover, Ananias's deceit was not due to a momentary lapse; it was a premeditated plan, to which his wife was a willing partner. The church was thus in danger. Such evil leaven would soon leaven the whole lump.   Insincerity and hypocrisy are fatal to vital religion and disastrous to missionary zeal. All the apostolic writers warn us against it. And, as we see in this incident, ' the love of money is a root of all kinds of evil.'

Exemplify this from any of the letters to the seven churches Asia. Rev. 2; 3.

Collect and compare references to money in Acts 2; 3; 8; 13; 15 and 19.

God's over-ruling grace is, however, again in evidence. Hypocrisy was checked; the work went forward; multitudes of new converts were gathered in; and the power of the gospel was felt far beyond Jerusalem. Once more the clouds broke; wrong was worsted; Christ and His cause were triumphant.

Give references which bear out these statements.

The next attack was delivered from **outside** the church, in the form of actual persecution. The continued progress of the work excited the adversary to try more determined measures. All the apostles, this time, were cast into prison, and afterwards accused before the Sanhedrin. Their bold testimony there cut the Sadducean party to the quick. It was seriously contemplated whether they should all be put to death. Only Gamaliel's intervention, under God, averted the catastrophe and saved their lives.

As it was, peremptory commands were laid upon them, and they were cruelly and severely beaten. Ridicule, questioning and threatening were thus succeeded by blows, wounds and bruises. We note, however, that the Lord was with them. He opened their prison doors and raised them up a friend in the camp of the enemy.

The history of missionary work holds many a record of persecution, imprisonment and stripes. Stern, of the London Jews' Society, and his companions were thrown into prison by King Theodore of Abyssinia in 1863 and kept in miserable captivity for five long and weary years, indignity and cruelty being heaped upon them. They endured untold horrors with the greatest courage and patience, and were the means of the conversion of some of their fellow-prisoners and jailers. Their sufferings terminated only when they were set free on Easter Day, 1868, by Lord Napier of Magdala and his troops, ' a resurrection festival indeed ', as Stern wrote, ' a foretaste of that glorious resurrection when decay and mortality shall be exchanged for life and everlasting beauty '.

Similarly, Ramseyer and Kühne, with the former's wife and child, languished and

3 PERSECUTION
(5 : 17-42)

How many stripes were usually inflicted ? See Dt. 25; and find a text in 2 Cor. bearing on it.

Cite promises to that effect from the Gospels.

suffered in prison for four years in Ashantee. The Glovers were stripped, insulted and mauled during the Boxer Riots in China. A council was held by their persecutors to take away their lives, and there seemed only a step between them and death. ' Oh ! father ! mother !' said their frightened children, ' are they going to kill us, really to kill us?' It was then that the heroic mother made them repeat, ' I will trust and not be afraid,' till the children fell into calm sleep; and that the father heard a voice from heaven, ' When thou passest through the waters, I will be with thee; and through the rivers, they shall not overflow thee.' Though they eventually escaped from their captors, Mrs. Glover and one of the children afterwards died of a disease occasioned by the hardships they had undergone.

Every mission-field can furnish illustrations of bitter persecution. Some years ago, a young Brahmin was baptized at a South Indian Missionary College. After his baptism, he was seized by means of guile, gagged, thrown face downwards in a cart and carried off to his Hindu home, where he was closely confined for six months in an inner room, and placed on short allowances of food. Everything was done which force or guile could suggest to shake his faith and resolution. When he slept, the mark of Vishnu was painted on his brow, only to be wiped off indignantly when he awoke. God was with him in that inner prison room, and his faith was sustained by a copy of the Bible which had been taken from him formerly but which he discovered secreted in a box. When at last he managed to effect his escape, and was asked what it felt like in that Hindu home, he said, ' I never knew till now how dark it was.'

Another time, a Brahmin youth who took up the cross to follow Christ was subjected to every kind of ill-treatment and persecution. He was cursed by his own mother; struck and stunned by his elder brother; locked up in a small room at home, after repeated beatings; dragged off to a distant town and there kept under guard; bound by a chain, on his return home, which was secured by a padlock; thrashed again and again by his relatives in turn for hours, and otherwise molested and maltreated until he finally escaped and sought protection and liberty of conscience among Christ's people. Even then, his Hindu friends followed him and sought, by magic and by mesmerism, to get hold of him. When all their endeavours failed, they were forced to acknowledge, ' No means which we have tried have availed against the gospel.'

Here also, as we learn from the narrative of the Acts, God's over-ruling providence is seen. Stripes served only to fill the apostles' hearts with joy. New vigour was put forth in service. The growth of the church was greatly promoted (6 : 1). The banner of victory still flew.

Find as many references to joy in the Acts as you can.

Satan's fourth assault was made, like the second, from within the church. The very increase in numbers brought with it problems and dangers. The Hellenists or Grecian Jews, speaking the Greek language, reading the Greek Scriptures, and more or less affecting Greek customs, carried their ideals and predilections with them, on conversion, into the Christian community. They were the tolerant and progressive party. The Hebrews, or Palestinian Jews, on the other hand, were rigid and conservative, despising all things foreign and more than

4 DIVISION
(6 : 1-8)

proud of their exclusive customs.

It was inevitable that friction should arise; and in this the adversary found his special opportunity. He resolved to 'divide and conquer'. He stirred up jealousy and party spirit. The apostles were accused by the Hellenists of partiality. There arose the danger of a fearful rupture. Satan knows full well that a divided church is shorn of its evangelistic strength.

What other instances do you know in the New Testament of his using this device ?

His attack was met, however, with rare wisdom. The apostles showed true self-abnegation. They recognized in the attack a peculiar opportunity for promoting the efficiency of the work. The whole church followed the example of their patience and forbearance. Special confidence was reposed in the Hellenistic party. The sound of murmuring died away, and the spirit of love and unity prevailed.

How does this appear ?

One of Satan's choicest devices is to divide God's people. We see it in the church at home; and there are numerous examples of it in missionary work abroad.

God's over-ruling grace, nevertheless, was particularly conspicuous on this occasion. Unity, so far from being destroyed, was cemented. The missionary work of the church was strengthened and advanced. The number of Christians multiplied exceedingly. A great company of the priestly class were converted. Stephen and Philip, among others, were raised up as pioneers. Once more Satan over-reached himself. The flag of progress still led the van.

5 MARTYRDOM
(7 : 54-60)

As the history proceeds, the battle waxes hotter and fiercer. Satan is seen delivering his fifth and most cruel stroke, this time again from **without** the camp. Stephen had proved himself a doughty champion of the cross. He was a missionary endued with more than ordinary spiritual gifts. His arguments were irresistible. He was more than a match for the representatives of three continents. His very face reflected his Master's glory. When placed on his defence, his words shattered the idol of Jewish exclusiveness. His opponents became mad with rage. They rushed upon him like infuriated beasts; and, outside the city, stoned him till he died. Thus Satan sought to silence the brave voice which continued to testify and pray while breath remained. But, here again, he over-reached himself. Stephen, being dead, yet speaketh.

'We are not ignorant of his devices.' Again and again, he has wielded the ruthless sword of martyrdom. Witness Ignatius, Polycarp, Felicitas, Perpetua and the other victims of the early persecutions. Witness our own Alban, Latimer, Ridley, Hooper. Witness the Madagascar martyrs, thrown from the rocks. One of these brave men, before he was rolled in the fatal matting and hurled down the precipice, asked permission to stand up and view for the last time, from the summit, the country which he loved so well. He feasted his eyes for a few moments on the scene, and bowed his head in prayer. He was then rolled in the mat and dashed down the rock. As his body descended, he was heard singing praise to his Saviour.

Witness Bishop Patteson of Melanesia, John Williams of Erromanga, Bishop Hannington of Uganda, James Chalmers of New Guinea — these and many more. Chalmers had gone ashore at Dopima, with some companions, hoping to appease a crowd of natives who had gathered in canoes with bows, arrows, knives, and spears. He had

What was his five-fold endowment ? See RV.

How can we show this ?

so often succeeded in pacifying angry cannibals that he was hopeful of doing so once more. But it was not to be. He and his friend were suddenly struck from behind with stone clubs. He was then stabbed with a dagger, and his head was cut off while he was lying senseless on the ground. Afterwards his body was divided among the cannibals, cooked and eaten. So perished, for Christ's sake and the gospel's, one who loved the cannibals of New Guinea with a warm affection, and gladly laid down his life for their salvation.

But still as we read the story of Acts, God's over-ruling grace works on. The Master rose and **stood** to help His faithful martyr. He filled his vision with heavenly glory and his heart with perfect peace. His martyrdom proved only the signal for fresh advance (8 : 1-4). It led to the evangelization of all Judaea and Samaria — to the founding of the missionary church of Antioch — and to a world-wide propagation of the gospel. ' The blood of the martyrs is the seed of the church.' ' The law of missionary work is increase through suffering.'

QUESTIONS FOR FURTHER STUDY

1   What should be (a) the attitude, (b) the action of missionaries and their supporters in order successfully to fight and conquer the power and devices of Satan?

2   Show how God's over-ruling grace was in every case manifested over Satan's opposition.

3   Where in the Epistles does Paul (a) emphasize the importance of prayer in the face of obstacles and opposition, and (b) connect together persecution and joy?

4   Where, in the Acts, does Paul allude to antagonism and danger first from without, then from within the church ?

5   What light does this chapter give on the problems of (a) overlapping of missionary societies, (b) caste spirit in indigenous churches, and (c) the need of discipline in church organization?

3 A MISSIONARY CENTRE

I know that I have opportunities of usefulness at home; nevertheless, in heathen lands there is gross darkness and scarcely any gleam of light.

Thomas Gajetan Ragland

Before the narrative of the Acts has proceeded far, we find the centre of missionary enterprise transferred from conservative Jerusalem to Antioch of Syria, which became the real base of operations for the apostle of the Gentiles. The reasons for this change are easily discoverable.

(a) **Situation.** Antioch was, after Rome and Alexandria, the third city of the Empire, and was, practically, the capital of the East. It was situated almost in the angle formed by the abrupt meeting of the coastlines of Syria and Asia Minor, and so presented a natural centre of operations to missionaries passing from Judaea in the South to the countries of the West. It was conveniently approached by the caravan routes of the lands of the East, and also it was in easy communication, through its harbour of Seleucia, with the trade of the Mediterranean world. The great overland route, also, connected it directly with Rome itself (see chapter 1).

(b) **Population.** It had been built about 300 BC by the Greek monarch Seleucus Nikator in the spot where the river Orontes passes between the ranges of Lebanon and

C

Passages for study
Acts 11 : 19-30;
12 : 25 - 13 : 4;
14 : 25-28; 15 : 1-3;
15 : 30-41; 18 : 22,
23; Gal. 2 : 1-18.

Taurus, and named after his father Antiochus. There was, therefore, a distinct **Greek** element in the population, though the mass of the people were **Syrian,** and the culture and civilization of the city were pronouncedly Grecian. Yet as it was under the Empire, the capital of the province of Syria and the residence of the prefect or governor, its official tone was Latin, and a considerable number of **Romans** were found gathered there. It must be added that the Greek founder of the city had, for political reasons, planted there a colony of **Jews,** and that the growing importance of the city continually attracted fresh members of the Hebrew race. Thus the population was mixed in character and presented special opportunities for missionary work. A church planted in such a centre was likely to be liberal and cosmopolitan in spirit.

In Syrian Antioch, then, it seemed good to God's wisdom to found the great missionary congregation, the mother of all the Gentile churches. Its glory and influence continued long after the history of the Acts was closed. It was prolific in great men — Ignatius, the martyr-bishop; Lucian, the greatest scholar of his time, also a martyr; Theophilus, the apologist, to whom we owe the word 'Trinity'; Chrysostom, the 'golden-mouthed' preacher; and many more; while the famous 'School of Antioch' claimed theologians of world-wide repute, such as Diodorus of Tarsus, Theodore of Mopsuestia, and Theodoret of Cyprus.

Even to this day a large section of the Syrian Christians of Malabar look to the Jacobite 'patriarch of Antioch' as their ecclesiastical head. A good deal of obscurity attaches to the question of the first foundation of this Syrian church in Travancore and Cochin. They claim to derive their origin from St Thomas. However this may be, they can be proved to have existed there at least from the fourth century of our era. During the Portuguese domination, however, they were compelled by force to wear the papal yoke. At a later period a large section revolted and connected themselves with Antioch, or rather with the Jacobite patriarch who claims to represent that apostolic see, and became Jacobites, keeping up their connection with Antioch to this day. A considerable section, however, have reformed themselves, and styling themselves the 'Mar Thoma church' have now much in common with ourselves. As a purified episcopal church, they are advancing in spiritual life and missionary zeal.

We see, then, that in spite of later corruptions the church of Antioch has exercised a lasting impression on the world outside; and the Syriac versions of the Scriptures have spread light and truth far and wide. Clearly God's blessing rests on missionary-hearted churches. They are, to use a suggestive Tamil illustration, like the graceful coconut tree which drinks in water by its roots only to give it out to others from its head, sweetened and enriched, in the form of luscious juice, and it does not grow the poorer for its gifts. This being so, we shall do well to ask : What are the special characteristics of the church of Antioch, the first typical missionary church ?

As we have seen, the population of the place was mixed, comprising Syrians, Jews, Greeks and Romans. We see this feature reflected in the composition of the Antiochene church.

1 IT WAS A COSMOPOLITAN CHURCH

The evangelists from Cyprus and Cyrene,

themselves Hellenistic Jews, addressed their message here, for the first time, especially to ' the Greeks ' (RV), i.e. Greek-speaking Gentiles; ' and a great number of those that believed turned unto the Lord '. Among these would be both Greeks and Syrians, with, probably, a sprinkling of Romans. They represented, most likely, that body of Gentiles who had previously come under the influence of Judaism and were, in varying degrees, in touch with the Jewish synagogue.

What verses in the Acts and in Galatians show this ?

Do we know the name of any uncircumcised Christian who accompanied Paul from Antioch ?

They were not, however, for the most part circumcised. They have their modern counterparts in India, China, etc., in those who know much of Christ but have not crossed the rubicon of baptism. There were also Jewish converts in the church of Antioch. Thus the congregation was cosmopolitan in character and composition, and so well fitted to become a missionary community. Being catholic in spirit and sympathy, it could feel for, and yearn over, the whole wide world of men. The more diversified the elements gathered into a Christian congregation, the more likely is that congregation to become a missionary power. Racial or caste spirit is the death of evangelistic zeal.

Why did a large section of the church of Jerusalem constantly oppose Paul's work ? Give reasons from both Acts and Epistles.

Some years ago, in a certain district of South India, the major part of a congregation gathered in church for a Confirmation Service fled through the windows because the bishop insisted on candidates being brought there who were regarded by the others as unworthy, on social grounds, to join with them in worship. Those who resented the intrusion of their poorer brethren represented a well-to-do section of the community who had come to regard Christianity as almost their exclusive monopoly in that district. With such a spirit, they could scarcely yearn over all sorts and conditions of men.

While we deplore such things in others we ourselves need to beware lest, however unconsciously, national and racial pride hinder, through us, the progress of the gospel. A Tamil pastor once told how some of the leading members of his congregation, when he had gone to preach to some poor people whom they regarded as outcaste and unclean, threatened to burn down the houses of any of those despised folk if they dared to seek admission to the Christian church.

These facts are mentioned not as ordinary occurrences but as somewhat extreme instances of the way in which racial or caste feeling, in congregations drawn chiefly from one section of a community, may and does seriously militate against aggressive missionary work.

On the other hand, memory recalls how, at some large evangelistic meetings for Hindus, also in southern India, a number of speakers of various nationalities, but all united in Christ and all actuated with one common love to Him, testified, one by one, in various languages, to the reality of the salvation which they had found and enjoyed in Him. Tamils, Telugus, Ceylonese, Englishmen, Americans and Danes — all had one tale to tell of grace and joy realized in a common Saviour; and all had one desire to see others brought to the knowledge of His truth. To use an Indian illustration, when the rice-fields are full of ripening grain the little ridges which divide them into plots and sections are lost to view, and we see not a series of separate patches but one wide stretch of living green. Christian unity and missionary fruitfulness will be found to go together.

2 IT WAS A VIGOROUS AND PROGRESSIVE CHURCH

Find them in Acts 11; 15.

In what verses ? Why is this specially the case at Antioch ? What bearing has it on missionary work ?

Find the verses which show this.

From the very first, conversions were numerous there, and the community continued to grow and expand. In at least four verses of the Acts stress is laid on the increasing size of the congregation. Three distinct stages of expansion are indicated in its initial history (11 : 20, 21; 22-24; 25-26). All was life, vigour, progress; there was no stagnation or standing still. The ' hand of the Lord ' was put forth there in saving power, if not also in signs and miracles. The ' grace of God ' was seen there in changed characters and consistent lives. Emphasis, moreover, is purposely laid on the Saviour's **lordship** and His claim on the service of His redeemed ones. We see, as we read, that the three great marks of this church, in its first period of existence, are **conversion, continuance** and **constant increase.** It will be found that the missionary outcome of a church or congregation always depends on its spiritual life and vigour. Periods of quickening are epochs in missionary history.

Take, for example, the Church of England, and what has been called ' the missionary awakening.' Was not this the direct result of the Evangelical Revival of the eighteenth century ? When, again, the American evangelists, Moody and Sankey, held their evangelistic campaigns in Great Britain in 1882-83, one of the most practical and permanent effects was seen in a great deepening of the missionary spirit, especially among the youth of our universities. Students were led first to Christ and then to His missionary service. To quote a few definite examples, one Cambridge man who had been given to pleasure and horse-racing was led to yield himself and his means for the service of Christ in Africa. Another undergraduate, who had at first opposed the meetings of the evangelists, was so completely laid hold of by God's Spirit that he went back to his college rooms, tore up his pack of cards, poured out his wine bottles on the ground and declared himself a converted Christian. He became a missionary bishop in China. The famous ' Cambridge Seven ' were an outcome of Moody's work, since some of them owed their conversion and others their consecration, under God, to his influence. As these seven men went from college to college and from town to town, the fire of missionary enthusiasm was kindled far and wide.

The same phenomenon may be observed in many lands — spiritual quickening followed by evangelistic zeal. A young Tamil schoolmaster, after coming into a fresh experience of grace and power, was sent to work in a Hindu village. He laboured earnestly to win souls, with the result that the boys in his school began to forsake idols and to turn their hearts to Christ; while a number of the young men of the place, one by one, became Christians. One of these young men, a strong and vigorous youth, when asked what first influenced him to become a Christian, said, ' The schoolmaster used to follow me to my work in the fields and plead with me to seek the Saviour, till I could no longer resist the plea.'

3   IT WAS A WELL-INSTRUCTED CHURCH

Emphasis is evidently laid on this in Luke's narrative. He attaches great importance to the fact that the church was carefully grounded and established in Scripture knowledge and in all the doctrines of the gospel. No less than eight teachers are mentioned by name as playing an important part in its instruction, besides others whose names are not recorded. **Exhorting, teaching, prophesying** and **confirming** are all noticed in

Who were these eight, and what share had they in the training of the church ?

connection with this work of instruction and missionary equipment. Information about missionary work, also, was not lacking, as the enterprise proceeded.

Show this. What missionary meetings were probably held at Antioch ?

Ignorance of God's word and will and work accounts largely, in any congregation, for the absence of missionary interest and zeal. On the other hand, a clear knowledge of God's purpose, as revealed in Scripture, removes opposition, dispels apathy and rouses to evangelistic effort. The same effects often follow from a full knowledge of definite missionary facts. We see, therefore, the great importance of Bible study — and, in its place, of missionary information — to the formation and cultivation of the missionary spirit.

Quote instances of these from the Acts.

It was when the Moravian Brethren — a small community of earnest Christian people gathered together by Count Zinzendorf at Herrnhut in Saxony, after their emigration thither from Moravia — were carefully studying John's First Epistle, section by section, that they got such a vision of the wondrous love of God that their hearts melted and some of them were constrained to volunteer for missionary work in the West Indies, even though it might mean becoming slaves themselves, in order to evangelize the slaves. From that time forward, the flame of missionary zeal has continued to burn brightly among them, and we find them at work in some of the most lonely and difficult parts of the earth, among the snows of Canada and on the barren borders of Tibet, as well as in South Africa, Australasia and elsewhere. The number of their converts in the mission-field far exceeds that of their members in the home-lands, and they are a shining example in their simplicity and ardour to other Christian churches.

It is from congregations with a full and faithful ministry, such as was that of Charles Simeon at Cambridge, that come forth the Henry Martyns. Mackay of Uganda was right when he said, ' There can be no evolution without corresponding and previous involution.'

A somewhat dignified Tamil 'munshi' (language teacher) would for years have nothing to do with street preaching or open aggressive efforts. He was cold and careless as regards evangelistic work. Then came the time when he began to read ' The Life of Faith ' and to study his Bible. As he read and understood God's will, his whole attitude was changed. The fire began to burn. All his spare time was given now to the furtherance of the gospel. He was more than ready to take part in any effort for the salvation of souls. Ignorance gave place to knowledge, and carelessness to earnestness. One of the last scenes in his earthly life shows him standing before a Hindu temple, pleading with the heathen to accept the Saviour. Like Paul at Corinth, he was ' constrained by the word ' (Acts 18: 5, RV) to testify that Jesus is the Christ and Saviour.

' The disciples were called Christians first at Antioch.' So long as faith in the Saviour was confined to Jewish believers, there was no need to give them a distinctive name. They seemed to the world at large only a Jewish sect — a new ' synagogue ', so to speak.

At Antioch, however, things were different. Many of the heathen population saw their own friends and relatives embrace the new faith and join the new community. The prevailing tone of the church was not Jewish

4 IT WAS A WITNESSING CHURCH

but Gentile. The rapid extension of the gospel, too, shows with what earnestness its members bore testimony to their belief. They talked everywhere about Christ. He was the object of their faith and the subject of their conversation.

As Ramsay puts it, ' The term (Christian) attests that the congregation became a familiar subject of talk, and probably of gossip and scandal, in the city. The name " Christos " must have been the most prominent in the expressions by which the Greek brethren described or defined their faith to their pagan neighbours. So it came to pass that, whether in contempt or in pleasantry — or, perhaps, in a more serious vein — the heathen populace styled the followers of the Saviour " Christians ", men connected with Christ and belonging to Him.' As has been well pointed out, the word (' Christianoi ') is itself Greek, while the idea expressed in it is Hebrew and its form is Latin. It was destined to replace all other titles and to become world-wide in its application. As we have seen, it arose from the zealous testimony of the church. Home missions are the best preparation for foreign missions. Soul-winning work abroad must be preceded by soul-winning work at home. ' If I had the true love of souls, I should long and labour for those around me, and afterwards for the conversion of the heathen ' (Henry Martyn).

How often does it occur elsewhere in the New Testament, and in what connection ?

5 IT WAS A GENEROUS CHURCH

What was the prophecy, and what do you know of its fulfilment ?

The prophecy of Agabus led to earnest effort and liberal giving. The approaching Jewish famine roused the gratitude of the Antiochene Christians, stirred their sympathies, and opened their pockets. We are not to think of their collections as a sudden, impulsive and instantaneous subscription. Chronological considerations show that something like two years elapsed between the prediction and the actual distribution of corn in the famine-stricken districts. There was, therefore, a systematic and sustained collection of contributions for the good cause; and we have here the first instance, in Church history, of a congregation carefully and liberally subscribing funds for the welfare of people living in another land. Famine-relief has often played an important part in missionary work. It led to thousands of people putting themselves under Christian instruction in Tinnevelly in AD 1877. The missionaries had funds entrusted to them by friends at home for supplying rice and grain to the starving population. This was a practical aspect of Christianity which the most ignorant could understand and appreciate, and was the means of saving many lives. While the well-to-do among the Hindus did little or nothing to relieve those who were perishing of hunger, the missionaries and their Indian fellow-workers passed from place to place feeding the hungry, tending the sick, and taking care of the orphans. ' The conviction prevailed that while Hinduism had left the famine-stricken to die, Christianity had stepped in like an angel from heaven to comfort them with its sympathy and to cheer them with its effectual succour ' (Caldwell).

Cite other examples from the New Testament. See Romans and 1 and 2 Corinthians.

Even men who, from caste pride and other reasons, affect to despise the gospel, have to acknowledge the force of its philanthropy and love. In a conversation held with a Brahmin official some years ago, a man of rare intellectual attainments and holding a position of great authority, the talk turned on the claims of our Lord Jesus Christ. When asked what he thought about Christianity he said, with something of proud complacence, ' Oh ! it is very good; but all its best doctrines are contained in Hinduism. **We** have the higher wisdom and philosophy.' When asked again, ' But what about the love which is revealed in the gospel ?' he replied at once, ' Ah ! I confess you beat us there. Why ! If the car-festival were going on in this town today, and some pariah child were to get caught in its huge wheels, there is not a Brahmin in the whole place who would defile himself by taking hold of it to try to save it.' And then he went on to narrate how cholera had lately been raging in a low-caste quarter of the town, and, because he was required to furnish the government with statistics connected with the epidemic, he had gone there each night in the dark himself to avoid observation, none of his subordinates being willing to enter such a quarter for fear of caste-defilement.

6 IT WAS A WILLING AND OBEDIENT CHURCH

We mark the note of **consecration**. Either the ministers alone, as some think, or the Christians as a community received a new revelation of God's will while they were actively engaged in their Master's service and giving themselves, in some special way, to prayer and fasting. Possibly, they were seeking guidance as to further developments in the work. At any rate, it was when they assumed the attitude of willing consecration that the missionary call reached them.

The lesson is clear. We must be willing to **do** our Master's will, if we honestly seek to **know** that will. There is a close connection between consecration and the missionary call.

Some years ago a company of the Hill Arrians of Travancore sent a deputation to the nearest missionary asking that Christian teachers might be sent them. It happened,

Give other instances from the Acts of special missionary directions being conveyed to those found in this attitude of readiness. See chapters 9, 10, 16, etc.

just at that juncture, that a young Syrian Christian had been led, through the influence of an Indian clergyman, to consecrate his life to the Saviour's service. He had told the Master, on his knees, ' Whithersoever Thou sendest me I will go.' The missionary turned to him in the emergency and asked him to take up this new enterprise. But the emoluments were small, barely enough for food and raiment; and the place proposed was feverish and unhealthy. How could he go ? So the offer was declined. That night, however, he had no sleep. It was as though the Saviour looked at him reproachfully and said, ' Did you not profess to consecrate your life to Me and to be willing to go anywhere for My name's sake?' He could not resist that Voice. He yielded up himself anew to Christ, and the next morning expressed his willingness to go. And he went, with the result that almost the whole tribe on that part of the hills turned from heathenism and drunkenness to Jesus Christ. Was it not worth while ?

The **obedience** of the Antiochene church is equally noticeable with its consecration. The command laid on them was, ' Separate me Barnabas and Saul for the work whereunto I have called them.' It was their best and most beloved ministers who had to be parted with for God's missionary work. And they were given up at once, gladly and without demur. After further prayer and fasting, a valedictory meeting was held, the first of its kind, and the congregation laid their hands on the missionaries, as though to claim a share in their work and to appoint them as their delegates. They then ' dismissed ' them; or, as we may better render the words, ' they released them ' (from their work at Antioch) and ' bade them farewell '. Are we ready to give our best for God's work abroad, to ' release ' our best ministers, to part with our best friends and nearest relatives ? Are we prepared to give to this work, if Christ calls for it, the best of our own life, strength and vigour ? The Christians of Antioch continued to regard their ' own missionaries ' with special attention and regard, and intercourse and communication with them were well maintained. Here also they are an excellent pattern for us all.

Show this.

QUESTIONS FOR FURTHER STUDY

1 What do you consider constitutes a missionary ' call '? How is this opinion borne out by the various examples found in the Acts?

2 From the Epistle to the Ephesians and elsewhere, discover how many of the six characteristics mentioned in this chapter were to be found in the church at Ephesus.

3 Show from the Acts how a clear knowledge of God's purpose, as revealed in the Scriptures, dispels apathy and rouses to evangelistic effort.

4 What do you consider to be the special missionary qualifications and defects inherent in the Anglo-Saxon race? Apply the principles set out in this chapter in determining your answer.

5 Why do you think that ancient churches, such as the Coptic church in Egypt, and the Syrian church in South India, have exerted so little missionary influence during the last thousand years?

China s not to be won for Christ by self-seeking, ease-loving men and women. Those not prepared for labour, self-denial, and many discouragements will be poor helpers in the work. In short, the men and women we need are those who will put Jesus, China and souls first and foremost in everything and at all times.

Hudson Taylor

Paul was designated, by God's wisdom and grace, to be 'the apostle of the Gentiles'. His is the central figure in the history of the Acts. He was, undoubtedly, the prince of missionaries. The more we study his personality and labours, the more we are impressed with the grandeur of his character and the greatness of his work. We may well regard him as the **typical missionary**, God's great pattern for all those who are called to carry the gospel to foreign lands. While we fall far short of his attainments, and admire him, so to speak, from a distance, we shall yet do well to study God's ideal, as exemplified in a real man of flesh and blood, and to aim at approaching, in our measure, the standard thus set before us. This pattern may be studied from many points of view. We might concentrate attention, for example, on his methods of work, or on his care for the churches, or on his choice and training of fellow-workers.

The aim of this chapter, however, is rather to regard him as a missionary in the making, and to discover what sort of qualifications and equipment are to be desired and devel-

Passages for study
Acts 7 : 54 - 8 : 4;
9 : 1-31; 11 : 25-30;
22; 26; Gal. 1 : 11-24;
Phil. 3 : 1-11.

oped in those who undertake this enterprise. It will be found that the great apostle possessed both natural and spiritual qualifications for his special work. While the latter are, of course, all-important, the former are by no means to be ignored. A. M. Mackay wrote words of wisdom to all would-be missionaries : ' Bring with you your highest education and your greatest talents; you will find scope for the exercise of them all.' This does not mean that only the highly educated can be useful in the mission-field. ' God fulfils Himself in many ways.' He chose ignorant fishermen, as well as scholars like Paul and Luke, for the propagation of the gospel. But it does mean that those who, like the apostle of the Gentiles, possess unusual qualifications from the advantages of birth and education, will find ample scope for them all in missionary work.

1 NATURAL QUALIFICATIONS Dean Armitage Robinson said of Paul : ' Alike by birth and training he was peculiarly fitted to be the champion of such a cause. A Jew, born in a Greek city, and possessed of the Roman franchise, he was in his own person the meeting-point of three civilizations.' This witness is true, and gives us the clue to many admirable qualities in the apostle's life and work. It will suffice here to mention three of these :

(a) **Tenacity**. The Jews are remarkable, as a people, for tenacity of purpose and persistence in enterprise. They surmount obstacles, succeed in various undertakings, and survive persecutions. Driven from one country, they make their influence felt in another; there is no more wonderful phenomenon in history than the persistence of the Hebrew race. Now this quality of tenacity and perseverance is invaluable in missionary work; and we see it constantly displayed in the history of Paul. His was ' the purpose ribbed and edged with steel ' which nothing served to blunt or turn aside. Of course, it was strengthened and sanctified by divine grace; but the quality was there, part and parcel of the man's character.

We see it, before his conversion, in his conduct as a Jew. We see it, after his conversion also, in his conduct as a Christian. It stands out in his words. Some of the most purposeful sayings in the whole Bible are found in his speeches and letters. It is conspicuous also in his deeds. When he was once convinced of his special mission nothing daunted his courage or checked his determined persistence. It survived and surmounted plots, persecutions, perils, stripes, imprisonments, misunderstandings, ridicule, sickness, desertion by friends.

Give illustrations from Acts, Galatians and Philippians.

Show clearly what this was from passages of the Acts.

He ' followed the gleam ' of his grand vocation in spite of suspicious friends, supercilious sceptics, sectarian bigots, superstitious pagans, self-seeking worldlings, well-intentioned though mistaken fellow-Christians. Right on to the end, his was ' the glory of going on and still to be '. His favourite metaphor clearly expresses it. Men and women who lack this quality of ' stick-at-ability ', in some degree at least, will never make good missionaries. Patient endurance, in the face of obstacles and trials, is indispensable. It should be practised at home so as to stand the severer test abroad.

What was it ? How often, and where, does he use it ?

When the Rev. F. Coillard and his devoted wife opened up work among the Barotsi people in the Zambesi region, they encountered untold obstacles. Their journey thither, to begin with, was one long series of disasters — sickness among their followers, bullocks dying by the road, goods stolen,

D

and so on. And when they reached their destination and commenced their work, trouble after trouble followed. One of their fellow-missionaries proved unfaithful; crocodiles got their pigs and dogs, and hyaenas seized their goats. When their long expected stores arrived from Paris, box after box was found riddled by white ants, with all the goods destroyed; thieves forced their locks and stole their tents.

But Coillard could write, with calm resoluteness : ' Behind us, these waves seem but small things. God will grant to each of us not merely to hold on but to go from strength to strength '; and his wife could write : ' We have never been so happy in mission work before.' When, again, they had erected their new house, with infinite pain and trouble, and, to their dismay, it was seen on fire a few days later, Coillard looked round to see what he could save from the burning wreck and cried, ' We must save the harmonium, for we shall yet live to sing !' His letters home are most inspiring all along; and both husband and wife held on bravely to the end and lie buried under a great tree at Sefula in Barotsi-land.

(b) Versatility. Though a Jew by race, Paul was born and bred in Tarsus, where Greek culture, society and institutions were in vogue. Its university was one of the intellectual centres of the Empire and famous for its teachers of the Stoic philosophy. We know that the apostle was more or less acquainted with the Greek poets and philosophy. We also know that his family enjoyed the privilege of the municipal or city franchise, i.e. the Greek citizenship of Tarsus, a privilege confined to a comparatively small section of the population. He had, therefore, imbibed a good deal of the Greek spirit — a

Do you know any of his quotations from the poets ? See Acts 17; 1 Cor. 15; Tit. 1.

Show this, from Acts 21.

spirit characterized by great versatility and readiness in resources; the Greeks were able to adapt themselves with ease to their surroundings.

This quality is strikingly present in Paul. He was equally at home with Jew, proselyte and Gentile. In his company of fellow-workers could be found the Asiatic, the European and the Eurasian. He could speak, as opportunity occurred, to Hebrew theologians, pagan idolaters and cultured philosophers; and his words were always suited to his hearers. His speeches before civil authorities show a clear knowledge of their character and history.

How does he refer to it in 1 Cor. 9 ?

Give names and proofs. Refer to Acts 4; 13; 15; 16; 19; Gal. 2; Col. 4; etc.

He could adapt himself with ease to the work of witnessing to all sorts and conditions of men — be they councillors, soldiers, sailors, ministers of religion, Roman officials, men or women. While he never ceased to be a patriotic Jew, he yet proved himself to the peculiar circumstances and position of Phrygian, Lycaonian, Asian, Macedonian, Grecian, Melitan and Italian.

This quality, again, is most useful to the missionary, and the absence of it accounts largely for the want of sympathy often observed between the foreign worker and those to whom he ministers. European reticence, rigidity and seeming haughtiness need to be watched and modified. We should cultivate the capacity to understand the attitude of men of alien lands and creeds; and we should learn to insist as little as possible on our own national customs, systems and church methods.

Here are two illustrations of the benefit of adaptation to circumstances. In scene number one, a very earnest Syrian Christian is seen, from our seats in a ' wallan ' (boat) on a Travancore river, to be following, on the river-bank, in the wake of a very dignified Jacobite, evidently burning to speak to him about salvation. We are near enough to land to hear what is being said. How will our friend get into close contact with the stately person whom he longs to tackle? Presently we hear him monotoning, as he walks behind the man, the Nicene Creed! The effect was evident. Even the most rigid of Jacobite Christians was satisfied with such a proof of orthodoxy. His hearer's attention was secured, and our friend then proceeded to speak of man's need of a personal Saviour. He had adapted himself perfectly to the position and attitude of the man whom he longed to help.

In scene number two, a large gathering of Hindus is being held in a large hall, and a good number are assembled. They are orthodox as to national costume, their feet being bare and their clothing confined to a long white loin-cloth, with a graceful piece of muslin thrown over the shoulder. They are Hindus of the Hindus, and their vernacular is Tamil. A convert has been asked to speak to them, a man of considerable parts and with a real experience of God's saving grace. But he has been brought up in a somewhat European style, and this is reflected in his dress. It was suggested to him that, in order to meet the conditions of the audience, he should doff his foreign garb and dress for the occasion in the usual Tamil style. He gladly acquiesced, and borrowed the correct 'dhoti' and shoulder cloth. And now he is standing on the platform to address the audience, one of themselves as regards dress and outward appearance.

He holds the people spell-bound, as he quotes stanzas from the Tamil classics in illustration of his points, and tells them, in glowing language, the story of his conversion. He stands there, an Indian of the Indians, and his clear words ring through the hall : ' Friends, we are Indians, the children of the " rishis " (sages and devotees) who tried to find out God and the way of access to His presence. That way now stands open and revealed in Jesus Christ.' For two nights they hung upon his words. He knew how to adapt himself, both in appearance and in language, to his audience, and the effect was striking.

(c) Practical ability. In addition to his Hebrew tenacity and his training in Greek culture and versatility, Paul derived distinct advantages from his Roman citizenship. This is to be clearly distinguished from the Greek franchise of the ' free city ' Tarsus, and was a far rarer privilege for foreigners to enjoy. It gave him a special status, and frequently procured him the friendship and protection of the imperial officials. It made him a member of a great body politic, one characterized by its grand ideal of universal empire and its power of organization. In this way, to use modern language, the apostle learned to ' think imperially '. Under the guidance of the Holy Spirit, he became a missionary statesman, occupying strategic points, moving upon lines of vantage, conceiving and developing a magnificent plan, ' the Empire for Christ '.

The Romans were noted for their organizing power and practical ability. They made great roads, established a settled peace, promoted facilities for trade and intercourse, carried everywhere a system of law and order. We find abundant traces of Roman influence in Paul's work. ' There had passed into his nature something of the Roman constructiveness, the power of seeing the

What passages of the Acts state this citizenship ? What use did he make of it ? In which Epistle is it specially reflected ?

Can you give instances from the Acts ?

means to reach an end in the world of reality and humanity, the quickness to catch and use and mould the ideas and ideals of the citizens of the Empire' (Ramsay, 'Pauline Studies'). His great conception of the evangelization of the Empire is definitely expressed in one of his Epistles.

Find it out in Rom. 15.

His conviction of the importance of organization, as also his promotion of it, is clearly evidenced in both Acts and Epistles. No-one is more decided as to the need of solidarity or organic unity, a principle which Rome aimed at but failed actually to achieve. Again, his practical nature and commonsense ability are seen in his choice of Silas and Timothy as fellow-workers, in his deterring the Philippian jailer from suicide, in his plan of special collections in the Gentile churches dispatched by trustworthy delegates, in his dealing with the plot against his life (chapter 23), in his conduct on board ship (chapter 27) and in his lending a hand to make a fire at Malta.

How does this appear, for example, in Acts 14; 20; 1 Tim. ?

Such qualities are most serviceable in missionary work. Many a missionary has to act, at times, as organizer, accountant, builder, doctor, and so on. An all-round knowledge of practical things may be turned to good account. When a large new bell from England, ordered for the Mengnanapuram Church in Tinnevelly, was found cracked on arrival, the Rev. John Thomas, a man of unusual practical ability, with the 'Encyclopaedia Britannica' for his guide, set to work to recast it with the help of Indian artisans, and succeeded perfectly. We have not all got his genius for mechanics, but we may all cultivate, with God's help, the application of our knowledge to practical things.

When a terrible epidemic of cholera broke out in a village of South India, the Christians of the place begged for special prayer. Their clergyman found, on his way to church, that there was a large cesspool standing right in the centre of the village, foul enough to account for any epidemic. He pointed it out to the people, and begged for something to be done. That was far too practical for them. They were ready for any amount of prayer, but not for the labour involved in filling up that awful pool. Not for one moment would we depreciate prayer. We need far more of it, but prayer and practice must go together.

Natural qualifications, however useful in their place, are of no avail in themselves for spiritual work : they will not bring the world into captivity to the obedience of Christ. Paul, however, was rich also in spiritual endowments for his special work.

2 SPIRITUAL EQUIPMENT

(a) Scripture knowledge. The ' sword of the Spirit ' is the Word of God, and this prince of missionaries was ' mighty in the scriptures '. He owed his knowledge of the Old Testament, of course, to his thorough training as a pious Jew. Though his family lived at Tarsus, a city of the Gentiles, his early religious education was carefully attended to. Afterwards, as a young man, he underwent a full course of theological instruction in Jerusalem, and became versed both in the Scriptures and in the religious literature of the Jews, being distinguished above all his fellow-students.

What passage of the Acts show this ? Consult RV.

Show this from Acts and Galatians. What other instances of early Scripture instruction occur in the New Testament ?

After conversion to Christ, the Bible, as he knew it, became an illuminated Book; and his Scripture knowledge, thus lit up, proved a mighty weapon in missionary work. He used it with convincing power in the various synagogues, in persuading Jews and proselytes and inquirers that Jesus is

Write down a list of these synagogues, as mentioned in the Acts. What was the result in each case ?

the Christ. His speeches on such occasions display a familiar and thorough acquaintance with the sacred writings and show plainly the object he had in view in citing them. When he stood on his defence, he appealed to the authority of Holy Scriptures. (See Acts 26.) He counselled his fellow-ministers to make God's Word their rule of life and doctrine.

Show this from Acts 20; 1 Tim.; 2 Tim.

In short, his history shows conclusively the necessity to the missionary of a sound and thorough knowledge of Bible truth. This it is which, applied by the Spirit to the hearts of men, both convinces the unconverted and also confirms converts in their faith. Ragland of Tinnevelly struck a true note when he wrote to a missionary designate : ' Let your preparation be the study of God's Word, your own heart and the hearts of others.'

What passage of the Acts shows this ? See chapter 18.

A few years ago, a young evangelist of South India was used in kindling the flame of what seemed like religious revival in many places. Men who were at variance with each other withdrew their lawsuits from the courts and made up their quarrels. A wave of fervent prayer swept over the congregations of that district. It looked as though a mighty movement were springing up. And then it all suddenly fell dead. What was the reason? The sword used was not ' the sword of the Spirit '. There was no instruction from God's Word at the meetings. The evangelist, though full of fervour, was ignorant of the Bible and did not know how to lead the people to base their faith and zeal on God's own truth. The consequence was an effervescence for the moment, followed by greater stagnation than before. We cannot attach too much importance to a careful study of the Word of God.

Some years ago a copy of the Bible in the vernacular was presented to every Hindu schoolmaster in a certain district of South India. Among others, one Hindu accepted a copy in order to find in it difficulties with which to confuse the donor. But he reckoned without his host. His questions were easily answered by one who knew his Bible well. This led the Hindu to a more serious and careful study still. As he read, the truth laid hold of him. He became a Christian, and then set to work to win others for his Saviour. He was the means of the conversion of quite a company of respectable Hindus, amongst them being the Brahmin priest of the temple in his native town.

(b) Spiritual life. The apostle's history, as a pious Jew, is proof positive of the fact that it is possible to be ' religious ' in an eminent degree, and yet to be destitute of real spiritual life. We cannot fail to be struck by the emphasis which is laid in the Acts on the **conversion** of the future missionary. We have no less than three separate accounts of it, and Luke is not in the habit of wasting words.

Paul himself refers to it, again and again, in his Epistles, foving to dwell on it with warm and glowing gratitude. To him, it was the real starting-point of his life and the first great preparation for missionary work. ' Life first; then service ' is a rule plainly exemplified in his history. And this life, imparted at conversion, was continually maintained, nourished and replenished. Neither the fatigues of travel nor the friction due to constant opposition availed to interrupt or retard it. It flowed on and on, deeper and fuller all the time. In one grand passage, in

Search out references in Gal.; 1 Cor.; Phil.; 1 Tim.; etc.

In which chapter
of Acts ?

What episodes of
the Acts prove this,
and in what
connnection ?

When ? Where ?

Cite instances from
2 Cor.; 1 Thes. and
elsewhere.

particular, he gratefully acknowledges the grace of continuance.

The secret of it is not far to seek; it lay in his habit of constant communion with his God and Saviour. We have dwelt already on his Bible study. We know him also to have been a man of prayer. On certain definite occasions he is seen retiring from the company of others to hold private communion with God. In seasons of sickness and trial, he went again and again to the throne of grace.

The reality of a man's faith and spiritual life is nowhere so severely tested as in the mission-field. Only those who are thoroughly converted, and know how to derive life and grace direct from God, ought to embark upon this work. But to such, missionary life brings rich opportunities, ' a more real blessedness in a lonely place, and with less of outside sympathy, which makes all the more room for His ' (Mrs. Polhill Turner).

Ragland of Tinnevelly has already been mentioned in this book. Though it is many years since he passed away, his memory still lives as that of one in whom the life of Christ flowed freely. We were once told by some Hindus how they came across him as little lads. He had pitched his tent in their village, and their sharp Indian eyes soon detected in him a holy man of God. They thought, however, that they would like to put him to the test; so, when they saw him sitting at his table, with his back to the tent door, they crept silently behind and stuck a pin into him. There was a sudden start. ' Well ! What did he say or do to you? Was he very angry?' ' Oh, no,' they replied, ' he only turned and smiled.' The lads were satisfied. They had found a man whose spiritual character could stand the test.

(c) Spiritual power. Spiritual life, for God's missionary, must be supplemented by spiritual power. Before entering on evangelistic work, Paul was ' filled with the Holy Ghost '. Without this special endowment, he could not be a successful worker. The power to win souls does not lie in natural advantages or intellectual ability, however useful these may be. It is a divine power, and is absolutely indispensable to the true missionary. Only ' that which is born of the Spirit is spirit '.

What verses state this ?

What texts in Acts 1-7 bear this out ?

It was in the power of the Spirit of God that the apostle entered upon his foreign work, defeated the forces of darkness, formed his plans of action, moved great cities, chose and appointed ministers, proclaimed the word of salvation. He realized fully, and taught explicitly, that without the Spirit's enabling grace, no man can either apprehend the gospel, accept the Saviour, or live a holy life. His letters reiterate constantly the indispensable necessity of receiving the Holy Spirit for assurance of salvation, victory over sin and certainty of coming glory (see Romans; Galatians). When addressing fellow-workers, he lays stress on the Paraclete's authority and work (see chapter 20). The book of Acts is full of the Spirit. We meet His name on almost every page, it confronts us at every turn, and Paul's missionary history is a clear picture of the working of His energy and grace. Every worker, at home and abroad, ought to be filled with the Holy Ghost; but His almighty power is nowhere more sorely needed than in the mission-field. We are face to face there with the powers of darkness in their most acute forms.

Establish each of these statements from the Acts.

Show this from 1 Cor. 1; 2; 6; 12.

Look at that crowd, for instance, gathered

round a devil temple for their annual festival. The image of the demon, a monstrous shape representing a woman treading one child under foot and holding another to her mouth ready to devour it, has been decked with garlands. Many goats have been slain before the shrine, and the blood of some of them drunk warm, as it flowed from the gashed necks of the victims, by the devil dancers. The weird music, discordant and wild, goes on and on. Several devil dancers, who are supposed to have received the afflatus, are whirling round and round to the strains of the music, faster and faster as the time is quickened. One of the dancers is a woman, with her hair dishevelled and flowing down her back. There is a frenzied look in her excited eyes as she dances frantically round and round. Some of the spectators look on awed. Others seem careless and indifferent. Many have brought their offerings, for they seek in this way recovery from sickness, rain for their crops, or relief from some malignant influence. It is a scene, once witnessed, never to be forgotten; but it represents the religion of tens of thousands in South India. Satan and his evil spirits seem, in such surroundings, to rule and reign.

Who is sufficient to cope with such things, but God Himself? Is not our Lord's command reasonable, and more than reasonable, from the point of view of missionary work, ' Tarry ye in this city, until ye be clothed with power from on high '?

QUESTIONS FOR FURTHER STUDY

1 Why is Paul considered a pattern missionary and what was the chief secret of his success?

2 Study the apostle's Scripture knowledge as shown in one or more of the Epistles of his Third Journey (Romans, Corinthians, or Galatians), noting

the passages from the Old Testament which he quotes or to which he refers.

3 Note Paul's personal prayer life, making a list of the things for which he prayed, (a) as regards himself, and (b) as regards others.

4 From a study of this chapter and the Scriptures mentioned what qualifications, natural and spiritual, would you regard as essential in a volunteer for missionary work?

5 From the study of the lives of such missionaries whose biographies you have read, bring examples of the qualifications emphasized in this chapter.

5 A MISSIONARY CAMPAIGN

> *'Agonia'* — *that word so often on St. Paul's lips, what did it mean? Did it not just mean the thousand wearinesses . . . and deeper, the strivings, the travailings, the bitter disappointments, the 'deaths oft' of a missionary's life?*
> Robert Stewart

Passages for study

Acts 13; 14; Gal. 1 : 1-9; 3 : 1-5; 4 : 8-20; 5 : 1-14; 6.

Paul was what we call nowadays an itinerant missionary. His tours are described in what are usually termed his missionary journeys, and are full of interest and teaching. In this chapter, we shall study the first of his eventful journeys, seeking, in particular, to view it in relation to modern missionary experiences.

1 CYPRUS: A BITTER OPPONENT

After the sea-crossing from Seleucia to Salamis, the missionaries travelled through the island till they reached Paphos, the political capital and the residence of the proconsul or governor. And here occurred a battle royal. The governor was clearly interested in religion, as appears from the fact that Elymas the magician was attached to his suite, just as we often find a Brahmin astrologer connected with the court of the Indian prince today. He heard of the itinerants and sent for them to come and preach. Possibly his heart was yearning for a purer faith. Then came the tug of war. Elymas represented a system which had cast a spell over the Roman world, a blend of pseudo-science and sorcery with religious superstition. He was astrologer, exorcist, magician and

What other traces of this system occur in Acts ?

fortune-teller all in one.   Every motive of self-interest urged him to resist the gospel.

He was all the more dangerous an antagonist because, being a Jew, he could doubtless quote, or misquote, the sacred Scriptures.   In bitter earnest he withstood the Christian preachers.   The gospel and heathen magic contended for the mastery; and the issue was not doubtful.   The judicial ' mist and darkness ' which fell on the magician were an emblem of the eclipse of all such false and occult systems. The sorcerer was worsted; the gospel triumphed; the proconsul ' believed, being astonished at the teaching of the Lord ' (not merely at the miracle).

What other individuals resisted Paul's work and with what result ?

Modern missionaries are often withstood by similar systems.   These are sometimes championed by individuals whose one object is to stop Christian preaching.

Some years ago, a ' Hindu Tract Society ' champion fiercely opposed every effort to preach the gospel in a city of southern India. He held rival preachings close to the places where the missionaries and their helpers were proclaiming Christ in the streets, in order to excite the crowd against them.   He disseminated Hindu tracts and literature of a very obnoxious character, reviling our Saviour and His gospel and chiefly based on atheistic books imported from the West. He left no stone unturned in his efforts to exterminate the Christian religion, root and branch.   It is interesting to note how all this fury ended.   The Hindus of the town became tired of supporting him.   His supplies ran short.   He was compelled to come and beg his railway-fare home again from the very missionaries whom he had constantly maligned.

Many a missionary has had personal encounters with angry Buddhist orators, or Muslim antagonists, or Ayra-Samajists. We learn from Paul that the way to meet such attacks is to be ' filled with the Holy Ghost ' and to declare faithfully ' the teaching of the Lord '.

2 PISIDIAN ANTIOCH : A MIXED POPULATION

The missionaries travelled by sea from Cyprus to Perga, and thence by road to Antioch.   Their path lay over the rough Pisidian mountain lands, which were full of dangers and infested by brigands.   En route, they crossed the boundary of the Roman province of Pamphylia into that of Galatia, in which Antioch, Iconium, Lystra and Derbe were **politically** included.   Antioch really belonged, from a **national** point of view, to Phrygia, though it was popularly spoken of as ' Pisidian '.   Its population included many native Phrygians; a strong Greek element, since it was founded by the Grecian monarch Seleucus Nikator; a Roman contingent, for it was a Latin ' colony '; and a large number of Jews.   It was therefore a good seed-plot for the cosmopolitan gospel of Christ.   It was, moreover, under the Romans, the centre of government administration for the southern part of the Galatian province.

Can you find a proof from the Epistle to the Galatians ? What other references occur to his constitutional malady ?

Show that the sermon divides itself into these heads.

The missionaries appear to have been detained there by Paul's severe illness. Then followed his memorable sermon in the synagogue, of which the main heads were (a) a Saviour promised, (b) a Saviour provided and (c) a Saviour presented. This led to experiences which present distinct stages : (a) The instruction of a large number of inquirers, Jews and proselytes.   (b) The awakening of wide-spread interest among the Gentiles of the city.   (c) The opposition of the Jews, from racial and religious jealousy.   (d) The concentration, for the

first time, on work among the heathen.
(e) The spread of the gospel in the ' region '
or county of which Antioch was the county
town.   (f) The arising, in consequence, of
bitter persecution, ending in the expulsion
of the missionaries from Antioch and its
environs.

In this persecution, their Jewish opponents were assisted by the city magistrates
who were influenced by Gentile ladies, semi-
proselytes.   The preachers were, possibly,
beaten also by Roman lictors.   Racial
jealousy, on the part of the Jews, was the
determining factor in the opposition, this
time.   The main result of the work was that
' the first thoroughly Gentile congregation,
separate from the synagogue, was established at Pisidian Antioch ' (Ramsay).

Mixed populations, as at Antioch, contain
both violent opponents and willing hearers;
and it is generally racial jealousy and sectarian pride which determine the character of
the opposition.

Show, from the narrative, that each of these stages is clearly marked.

The missionaries journeyed from Pisidian
Antioch to Iconium along what was called
' the imperial road ', the distance being about
eighty miles.   Iconium was an important
commercial town.   Like Antioch, it was
Phrygian, from the **national** point of view
(though closely associated with Lycaonia).
Roman and Greek influence were not so
strong, by far, as at Antioch; but Jews were
numerous.   Some of the characteristics of
the work at Antioch were reproduced here
also.

The chief feature, however, emphasized in
the narrative is the fervency and vehemence
of the Iconians.   From the first, interest was
aroused, and division ensued, both among
Jews and Gentiles.   The synagogue was

3 ICONIUM: A VEHEMENT PEOPLE

Compare the two as regards work in the synagogue, labours outside the synagogue, and growing opposition.

E

moved and divided; so was a wider company; and so, at last, was the whole city. Everyone took sides; no-one was apathetic or indifferent. The town was ranged in two opposite camps. Those who were not for Christ were actively against Him; and the opposition united forces which normally worked in contrary directions. The hostile party, Jews, pagans and authorities, combined to foster a public riot, with murderous intent, and the missionaries retired from the place for the time being.

What verses of Scripture support their action in so doing ? From what other cities was Paul obliged to retire ?

What passages in the Epistles — e.g., 1 Cor.; 2 Cor.; Phil. — confirm this ?

Here, again, are features not uncommon in modern missionary work. The gospel often acts as a dividing force. Some of us have seen whole towns or villages ranged round the Hindu (or Buddhist) preacher on the one hand and the Christian evangelist on the other hand. A mission school which produces converts is opposed by the opening of a rival anti-Christian school. When a young Brahmin student in one of our high schools came out for Christ, the whole town was divided. Some of the Hindus, partly from respect for the headmaster, partly from higher reasons, still held by the mission school; while the majority of the Brahmins and their followers, stirred up still further by the local Hindu lawyers, offered the most strenuous opposition and sent emissaries to every street to forbid attendance at the Christian school and to compel adhesion to its Hindu rival. The conversion of a second student, following almost immediately on the former one, only added fuel to the flame.

We may note, also, that incongruous elements sometimes combine, as at Iconium. During an open-air preaching to Hindus in a very bigoted country town, a troublesome objector stepped forth from the heathen crowd in the person of the local Roman

Catholic catechist who plied us with questions about the supremacy of Peter and the salvation of Protestants. It was not difficult to answer his questions; but it was sad to see that he would rather have men worship demons than accept our gospel.

Lystra was only eighteen miles south-south-west of Iconium, and was situated in a comparatively retired spot, some miles distant from the great overland route (see chapter 1). It belonged to that western part of the country of Lycaonia which was included in the Galatia province. It was a Roman 'colony', and so both Latin and Greek influence were present; but its population was mainly Lycaonian, comparatively uneducated and under the sway of crude pagan superstitions. Jews were few in number, as appears from the fact that no synagogue is mentioned there. A striking miracle of healing stirred to its depths the superstitious reverence of the people. They prepared to treat the missionaries as divine beings. A procession was formed, with oxen, garlands and the usual paraphernalia of idolatry; and the priest of Jupiter was on the point of offering sacrifice.

4 LYSTRA: A SUPERSTITIOUS COMMUNITY

Why did they give precedence to Barnabas? Why did not the apostles stop them at once?

It was only then that the missionaries rent their clothes and begged them to desist. Paul seized the opportunity to tell them of the true and living God, His unity, His omnipotence, His patience, His beneficence, His invitation, His gospel. It was just such an address as a missionary might give under similar circumstances today. Those who know what heathen processions are, with their musical accompaniments, noise and excitement, can appreciate Luke's words, 'scarce restrained they the multitude'.

Trace these points in his address. How would you meet the objection that there is, apparently, nothing in it about Christ and salvation?

Superstitious people are generally excitable and somewhat fickle. Jewish emissaries from Antioch and Iconium easily perverted their minds and persuaded them to allow Paul to be stoned. He was, however, miraculously preserved from death. Possibly, this new miracle once more overawed them, for he was allowed to spend the night there and to depart quietly next day. He left converts behind, and so his sufferings were fruitful for the cause.

How many miles had these emissaries travelled, and how many times were attempts made upon Paul's life ?

Find proofs of this statement.

The story of Lystra is often repeated, in its main features, on the mission-field. A scene is vividly present to our mind, when, having gone to preach in a large village, we saw a heathen crowd approaching in procession with music and drums. They were carrying, as an offering to their temple, the first shoots of their springing crops, to propitiate their god and to ward off his envy and anger. When they caught sight of a white face, they gathered around us, as we stood on a sort of raised platform, made the most profound ' salaams ', and were ready to show us the utmost deference. Possibly, they feared that our presence might interfere with the merit of their special offerings unless they placed themselves on good terms with us. Anyhow, they stood and listened while we read to them this very account of Paul's address to a similar pagan procession at Lystra and pleaded with them to ' turn from these vanities unto the living God '.

5 DERBE: A QUIET AUDIENCE

Derbe was thirty miles south-east of Lystra, and was situated on the main highway of travel. It was a frontier town, on the border of the Galatian province. Beyond it lay a large native state. Its importance consisted chiefly in its frontier position. The fact that Paul journeyed there the very day after the cruel stoning shows, of itself, the miraculous character of his recovery. The work in Derbe seems to have been like a calm after a storm. Doubtless, much more happened there than appears in the narrative; but the impression left on the reader is that there was no violent opposition. They ' preached the gospel there ' and ' made many disciples '. Similarly, the missionary of our own days often finds an audience prepared to listen to his message, even though they may not be eager to accept it.

Do we know any of these by name ?

Some years ago we found a village in Tinnevelly in a similar attitude of receptivity. Every house we visited was filled with a willing audience, and the whole village gathered to the torchlight preachings by night. The result was a Christian congregation which has been constantly receiving additions ever since. Truth, however, compels the statement that such a spirit of ready receptivity is the exception rather than the rule; and it is often from more opposing places that the best converts are won.

Paul and Barnabas did not cross the Roman frontier and return to Syria by the ' Cilician Gates ' (see chapter 1). It may have been too late in the year to cross the mountains by that route. More probably, they were actuated by a desire to consolidate the work so happily begun. They returned, therefore, to Perga via Lystra, Iconium and Antioch. Their work in the new churches assumed a four-fold shape : confirmation (of faith), exhortation (to continuance), ordination (of ministers), and commendation (to the Lord). Every missionary knows the importance of attending to these matters in infant churches.

Show the meaning of each of the four, and the necessity. On what other occasions did Paul revisit these churches, and why ?

Thus evangelization was followed by organization, and the newly-lit lamps were left, so to speak, trimmed and brightly burning.

QUESTIONS FOR FURTHER STUDY

1 What points, specially mentioned in Paul's missionary commission given at his conversion (compare the various accounts), are illustrated in this narrative?

2 Relying on the authority of Acts 13 and 14, how would you meet the following statements? :
   - (a) Christianity is too spiritual a religion for the lower races : idolatry suits them better.
   - (b) The conception of one true and living God is the product of a slow evolution in the mind of man.
   - (c) So long as the life of Christ remains, we need not mind the destructive criticism of the Old Testament.

3 Had you been Paul's companion on this journey, which of the experiences recounted would have been especially trying to you?

4 What do we learn from Paul's example as to the comparative importance of evangelistic, medical, educational and pastoral missionary work?

5 Give modern examples of opposition to the gospel based on
   - (a) National and racial pride.
   - (b) Social prejudice.
   - (c) Ecclesiastical jealousy.

If any qualification seems necessary to a missionary in India it is wisdom, operating in the regulation of the temper and the due improvement of opportunities.

Henry Martyn

As missionary work proceeds, and converts are gathered in, problems of various kinds arise calling for wise solutions. We have examples of such problems in Acts, some connected with church contributions, some with pastoral oversight, some with the suitability or otherwise of workers, others with questions of conformity with national and religious customs, and others with missionary extension. The problem of problems, however, of that period was that of the admissibility of the Gentiles into the Christian Church on equal terms with Jewish believers, without distinction and without circumcision. In other words, it was the racial problem. It is not easy for us to realize the gravity and acuteness of the difficulty as it appeared to Jewish eyes. Christ was, in their conception, the Messiah of their favoured race. The Christian Jew was prepared to admit the Gentile believer to church fellowship, but only on condition that he entered through the door of circumcision and conformed to Mosaic institutions. To put it plainly, one of an alien race must become a Jew in order to become a Christian.

Hence, the battle raged round this question throughout the history of Acts. It

Passages for study

Acts 15 : 1-35; 21 : 17-25; Gal. 2 : 1-10; Rom. 3; Eph. 2 : 10-22; 3 : 1-10.

Give an instance, or instances, of each of these.

required a special revelation to induce even a leading apostle to believe that the door of God's mercy stands wide open to all believers. Even after such a revelation, Peter acted against his new convictions. To Paul himself, the free admission of the Gentiles was a stupendous 'mystery' or 'secret'. laid bare to him by God. Only by degrees did he himself grasp its real meaning. As it dawned more and more clearly on him, he obeyed 'the heavenly vision', at the cost of obloquy, persecution and personal liberty. The word 'grace' assumed a new meaning to him : it came to denote that 'surprising mercy of God by which those who had been wholly outside the privileged circle were now the recipients of the divine favour' (Dean Armitage Robinson).

In different forms the old problem still survives. We see it in the 'caste question' of India, which gives trouble even in the Christian church.

The problem in question, however, is by no means confined to caste distinctions in India. We meet with it also in the 'colour question' of America and in the 'native question' of South Africa. We 'whites' are far from guiltless in the matter. We are all slow to learn, in practice, that in Christ Jesus there is, and there can be, neither Jew nor Greek, neither American nor Negro, neither Englishman nor Indian. The watchword of the gospel is 'catholicity, not caste; solidarity, not race'.

1 THE CONTROVERSY (15 : 1-3)

When Paul and Barnabas returned from Galatia to Antioch, they related their experiences, and announced, in particular, that God 'had opened a door of faith unto the Gentiles' (14 : 27). This was the great feature of their first missionary tour. Clear-

---

Side notes (left margin):

When ? Where ? How ?

Show this, for example, from Acts 22, and compare his teaching in his letters to the Ephesians and Colossians.

Trace this new meaning of 'grace' in either Acts 11-28 or Ephesians, or both.

ly, it excited the utmost interest in the church of Antioch, many members of which were themselves converted Gentiles. It also provoked opposition from the circumcision party in Jerusalem, some of whom arrived upon the scene and vigorously contested the new departure. They insisted that Gentiles should be circumcised and keep the law of Moses. The point at issue was plain and definite; it was 'the door of faith' versus 'the door of circumcision'. Men were in earnest on both sides, and a sharp controversy ensued. There was 'no small dissension and disputation'. The problem was vital and must be solved. What steps were taken to that end?

Trace the attitude of this party in Acts 11; 21.

(a) **A conference was agreed upon.** The subject must be properly thrashed out, and, if possible, a satisfactory concordat reached. This was a wise determination, and one according to the mind of Christ. All such conferences are, surely, good and right.

We read of four Jerusalem conferences in Acts. What were they, and what did they consider?

(b) **Due regard was paid to corporate unity and order.** Both sides agreed to go 'unto the apostles and elders about this question.' This does not mean that the latter were regarded as a sort of papal and infallible authority. Paul was always careful to defend his independence, and would never yield to any man in vital matters.

Prove this from the Epistle to the Galatians.

(c) **The utmost reliance was placed on God's will and leadings.** The missionaries reiterated again and again what God 'had done with them' (14 : 27; 15 : 3, 4). Prejudice must yield to facts. In every phase of work, God's will must rule. It helped materially to an agreement that stress was laid not upon 'Pauline methods', but upon divine guidance and approval.

These three great principles, friendly conference, regard for corporate unity and order, and a clear setting forth of God's leadings and doings, will guard us, respectively, against needless division, excessive individuality and mutual misunderstanding in our work. Controversies have arisen, and still arise, over mission comity, methods of work, Church discipline, and so on. We still need to resort to the procedure described above.

2 THE COUNCIL (15 : 6-29)

It is assumed here that Gal. 2 : 1-10 refers to Paul's third visit to Jerusalem as described in Acts 15, though Ramsay and others refer it to his second visit.

The council proper seems to have been preceded by two important events. A futile attempt was made by the circumcision party to beg the question at issue by insisting on the circumcision of Titus; and a private conference was held between the missionaries and the heads of the church at Jerusalem. This cleared the air. When the council actually assembled, there was at first a sharp division of opinion and ' much disputing ' or ' questioning '. But the sound of altercation was soon hushed, and the forces of truth and love prevailed. We have here a model, in this willingness to cease from strife, for all Missionary Conferences, Church Councils and Ecclesiastical Synods. Memory recalls a gathering of workers in India at which there seemed likely to be a collision between the Indian members and the foreign missionaries, with the possibility of a strong cleavage of opinion calculated to lead to unhappy results. The crisis was met in the spirit of love on both sides, and the resolutions of the conference were practically unanimous. While it can never be right to yield a vital principle, it must always be right to meet differences of opinion in the spirit of love and to avoid, as far as possible, unworthy strife. Several features stand out prominently in connection with this council of Jerusalem.

(a) **The presence and guidance of the Holy Ghost** were expected, realized and acknowledged. They had met on His business and must act under His control. A deep consciousness of this will make a difference in all discussions and affect all decisions and conclusions.

Which verse proves this?

Which of His functions and gifts were most required?

(b) **The authority of Holy Scripture** was respected and submitted to; its testimony was accepted as decisive. It was shown clearly that the Old Testament had foretold grace and salvation for the Gentiles. Where the Bible, in its plain meaning, is acknowledged as the ultimate court of appeal, unity becomes possible. We met on one occasion in South India for an important conference, at which questions of policy had to be faced and decided on. It was known beforehand that different members held, and held strongly, views on the matters under consideration which seemed to be incompatible; and the chairman of the conference expected a somewhat heated altercation. The proceedings, however, opened with a Bible reading; and the words of God's Book laid hold of all present. When the discussion began, it found us all under that sacred influence, and there was no heated altercation but only friendly deliberation, with unanimous conclusions.

Show this.

(c) **The evidence of facts** was emphasized and honoured. This occupied an important place in the procedure of the council. Three at least of the four most prominent speakers dealt mainly with missionary facts. Theory and prejudice had to yield, when true witness was borne to God's will and work. What was the use of arguing about the position of the Gentiles under the new dispensation, when it was proved by reliable witnesses that God had declared for their

Who were they? What did they say?

admission on equal terms with His favoured people?

(d) The sufficiency of faith was insisted on and proved. One of the simplest creeds in the whole Bible is found in chapter 15. It was shown that it is faith, not circumcision, which produces purity, deeper purity than ceremonial observances can ever give. It was claimed that salvation is, on God's side, all of grace; and, on man's side, all of faith. In this really consists the great difference between the gospel and all the religions current among non-Christians. Those religions, one and all, offer their benefits as a reward for human works of merit. We, on the contrary, offer a full and free salvation, without any works of human merit, to every sinner who comes for refuge to the Lord Jesus Christ, trusting in His finished work.

These four outstanding features will help us, in any conference, to avoid the mistakes, respectively, of human combativeness, self-assertion, prejudiced judgment and insistence on non-essentials.

What is it ?

3 THE CONCORDAT
(15 : 19-20, 22-29)

The council, happily, arrived at a unanimous conclusion. A concordat was agreed upon which was satisfactory, for the time at any rate, to all concerned. This decree may be termed the Magna Charta of Gentile liberty.

(a) It declared for the door of faith, as against the door of circumcision, so far as the Gentiles were concerned. Admission to Christ, and through Him to His church, was pronounced to be by faith and faith alone.

(b) It acknowledged the abolition, in Christ, of all distinctions between Jew and Gentile. Noble words were spoken which were at least reflected in the letter of the council. It was stated that God ' made no distinction between them and us ', and that

Show how this is reiterated and worked out in the Epistle to the Galatians. Why in that Epistle ?

' we shall be saved . . . in like manner as they '. The wall of partition was broken down for ever. Those words ' making no distinction ' still ring on, and we need to act on them more fully in missionary operations.

Find the passage of Ephesians in which this wall is mentioned. To what does the metaphor refer ?

(c) **It pronounced in favour of liberty from ceremonial yokes.** The Jew had no right to impose his national and ecclesiastical customs and traditions on Gentile believers. They were not of the essence of the gospel. And we are warned hereby to beware of oppressing the infant churches of the mission-field with our own national rules and customs and ecclesiastical systems and accretions. We westerners often carry to eastern lands denominational shibboleths and church organizations which are not of the essence of the gospel. Very solemn were Peter's words, ' Why tempt ye God, to put a yoke upon the neck of the disciples?'

(d) At the same time, **it directed abstinence from certain evils and customs** common in the Gentile world. These are four in number, and may be regarded as dealing with two main socio-religious questions, food and purity, questions which seriously affected the intercourse of Jew with Gentile. While, to our eyes, three of these may seem to refer to ceremonial matters, and only one to a directly moral one, we have to remember that in heathen countries, the moral and ceremonial are closely interwoven, and that social and religious customs are practically inseparable. When the Hindu takes his morning bath in river or tank (lake), the whole proceeding is practically an act of worship to the sun. When he proceeds to his meal, he is expected, besides ceremonial ablutions, to offer a portion to the household gods; and even the ball of rice which he appears to throw in pity to the crows which

Find a further reference to this Mosaic yoke in the Epistle to the Galatians.

gather round his courtyard is really a sacrifice and bears that name. When the Hindu woman nightly lights her lamp, the act is associated with the worship of Agni, the god of fire. Even the ornamental chalkings on the ground outside her doorstep have a religious significance. We may look at the four points in some detail.

(a) ' Things sacrificed to idols ' were sold in the markets and eaten at ordinary household meals and social feasts by the Gentiles of those days. Even to this day, in India, one of the first points on which many a convert takes a stand is the refusal to touch food which has been offered, chiefly on festive occasions, to Hindu gods or demons. In particular, the Indian New Year is a great testing time with many. The family food in certain circles is cooked that day before the altars of the gods, and all are expected to partake freely of it. A refusal to touch it, on the part of one known to be interested in the gospel, is regarded as a confession of faith in Christ.

Where else are they mentioned ? See 1 Cor. and Rev.

Some years ago, the leading Hindus of a large town in the Tinnevelly District paid a visit of respect to the (late) Bishop of Madras, bringing garlands with them, bunches of plantains and other gifts. We had reason to think that some of these had previously been offered at the shrine of the god in the local temple. When challenged on the point, they acknowledged that this was the case. Of course, there was nothing to do but politely to decline their gift, explaining to them the reason. It would never have done to have sanctioned their idolatrous actions with our eyes wide open. As regards the Jews, there were definite prohibitions against it in the law of Moses. The Jews of the Dispersion, therefore, were

Find them.

careful to avoid it.

(b) 'Blood'. The Gentiles ate this, while it was strictly forbidden to the Jew, and that for sacred and doctrinal reasons. Devil-dancers in South India, when the afflatus is upon them, sometimes drink blood as it pours from the neck of a goat which they have slain before the shrine.

Find the passages which prove this, e.g., in Leviticus.

(c) 'Things strangled'. To the Jew, this would come under the category of Leviticus 17 : 13; he was not to eat any animal the blood of which had not been previously let out. The Gentiles, on the other hand, esteemed meat killed by strangling a special delicacy. It is for reasons such as these that that the Jews always had, and still have, butchers of their own. There is in all of us a natural feeling in favour of this third prohibition.

(d) 'Fornication'. In Paul's days, immorality formed part of the worship of many temples. The temple of Aphrodite at Corinth alone had attached to it a thousand 'slaves of the gods' who were public prostitutes. And in some parts of some countries today immorality and idolatry still go hand in hand; but we in the West have nothing to boast of, with sexual immorality engulfing thousands of our young men and women. There is certainly cause for this decree : in every land and in every church people need to be told in the plainest possible terms that sexual intercourse outside marriage is absolutely forbidden by the law of God.

The results of this missionary conference were great and far-reaching. We can enumerate only some of them, leaving the student to search the subject for himself.

4 THE CONSEQUENCES (15 : 30-35, 40-41; 16 : 1-5)

(a) The special missionary work of Paul received the imprimatur of the whole church.

Where did Paul have a 'glad surprise' in the shape of a new comrade, after starting on his next journey? Look out the 'glad surprises' of Acts, each ushered in by a sudden 'lo' or 'behold'.

(b) Peace, joy and comfort were promoted in the Gentile churches. (c) New missionaries were forthcoming for work among the Gentiles. (d) There was a fresh ingathering among the heathen. (e) The gospel was carried, without gainsaying, to new lands and provinces. (f) The cause of Gentile liberty was won, however much it might still be attacked from time to time by the circumcisionists. The flag of freedom had been raised aloft. It could never more be furled or taken down.

QUESTIONS FOR FURTHER STUDY

1 What special problems arose in the Corinthian church? How, and in what spirit, did Paul deal with them?

2 On what occasion, subsequent to the council at Jerusalem, did Paul conform to special Jewish usages? Was he inconsistent in what he did?

3 Show the importance of the Christian faith being presented to the native peoples in a form which they are able to appreciate, and with as few European customs, etc., as possible.

4 What light does the study of Acts throw upon the principle that a native indigenous church should be self-governing, self-supporting and self-with them?

BOOKS FOR FURTHER READING

Missionary Methods: St. Paul's or Ours?
The Spontaneous Expansion of the Church
The Ministry of the Spirit
by Roland Allen
(World Dominion Press)